**HOW TO DESIGN
THE PERFECT
MENU SYSTEM**

A Mise Mode Guide
to Fresh Food Menu Strategies
That Actually Work

HOW TO DESIGN
THE PERFECT MENU SYSTEM

RENEE GUILBAULT

●● PAGE TWO

Copyright © 2023 by Renee Guilbault

All rights reserved. No part of this book may be reproduced, stored in a retrieval system or transmitted, in any form or by any means, without the prior written consent of the publisher, except in the case of brief quotations, embodied in reviews and articles.

A Taste of Opportunity, Mise Mode™, and the planning tools referenced in this book are either registered or used by Essayer Productions LLC, DBA Essayer Food Consulting.

Some names and identifying details have been changed to protect private information.

Cataloging in publication information is available from Library and Archives Canada.
ISBN 978-1-77458-375-3 (paperback)
ISBN 978-1-77458-359-3 (ebook)

Page Two
pagetwo.com

Edited by Melissa Edwards
Proofread by Melissa Kawaguchi
Cover and interior design by Taysia Louie

essayerfoodconsulting.com

For Zachary Thomas,
my fave badass food developer.

CONTENTS

Welcome to the Complex
World of Fresh Food R&D *1*

1 **Know Your Menu, Know Thyself** *5*
2 **Keep That Menu Wheel Turning** *19*
3 **"Calories In, Calories Out"** *31*
4 **Let's Play Operations** *41*
5 **Care for a Case Study?** *53*

A Closing Note:
Why What You Put on Your
Menu Really, *Really* Matters *63*

Spiced-Apple French Toast
(for on the GO!) *65*

Tools and Resources *67*

WELCOME TO THE COMPLEX WORLD OF FRESH FOOD R&D

LET'S CUT TO THE CHASE, because anyone who is running or launching a fresh food brand does not have time to waste. *Right?*

There is only one way a food business can stay in business, and that's through selling—*profitably* selling—food and drink. If the items you put on your menu don't drive sales or the cost of producing and selling them is more than they earn, guess what's going to happen? That's right—big trouble in food paradise.

Using your menus as a strategic system designed for success instead of a curated list of dishes is the difference between stellar financial performance and meh. That means the most powerful tool you have to drive successful performance and ensure longevity is your menu.

The menu your customers (or future customers) are reading in your restaurant or online has more of an effect on people than you might know. Each item you choose to feature has the ability to make one person's meal delightful or disappointing, nourishing or draining, forgettable or—for good reasons or bad—mind-blowingly memorable. With each dish you design, you have the opportunity to create a conversation, a trend, even a game-changing movement. No matter the size of your business, you can create awareness around everything from ingredient provenance to responsible waste disposal with subtle messaging and intentional word choices. And, of course, the dishes you present on your menu are deciding the future of your business itself: every single item might just be the thing that makes or breaks you in real time.

I've been responsible for overseeing the food teams that create new menu items and manage menu launches for massive brands and corporations across my career (I mean *massive*—think major restaurant names you might see on the daily, serving 60,000 meals a day and more), and if you were introduced to my Mise Mode methodology by reading *A Taste of Opportunity,* you already know how I feel about food—especially fresh, nutritious food and the importance of putting dishes on menus that are designed to delight, to nourish, and to drive profit and revenue. Now, I want to help more food businesses—from the chains to the independent restaurant operators—understand and adopt the real systems and strategies that make it possible for the world's major fresh food brands to navigate the many, many challenges this industry throws at you, and create delicious, good-for-you, and *profitable* menus that people actually want.

This, right here, is the ultimate purpose of Mise Mode, my career-development version of the mise en place that most professional chefs use in the kitchen to make sure everything they need is prepped, organized, and in one place before they start cooking. Except in this case, your mise "bowls" are the planning tools, strategies, and even mindsets I lay out in this book—plus some takeaway summaries that will help you boil down the lessons of each chapter into a few key ideas you can use right away to start designing and managing your menus like a pro. You are about to reap the benefits of all the best processes and strategies I've created and used over the long years I've spent in this industry working with a wide range of food organizations. There are a lot of factors to consider in this Mise Mode framework, but it begins with one thing: understanding how important good, adaptable menu planning is to the success of a fresh food brand.

There Is No "Random" in a Successful Fresh Food Restaurant

Fresh food R&D is a whole different beast from the mass manufacturing world—one that's easier in some ways and *faaaaar* harder in others. In the mass production universe, R&D teams require a year (at least) to develop a new product and get it on the shelf, and that's in the simplest scenarios—two big reasons for this long time frame are the supply chain and logistics considerations that big manufacturers face, and because they need to do all their testing behind the scenes. But when you're working in the more agile world of fast-casual, multi-unit fresh food restaurants, a product idea can be in a diner's plate in as little as 12 weeks. It's an *extraordinary* advantage—you can real-world test and get feedback immediately, and you don't have to commit to any product for longer than a quarter, a month, or even a couple of weeks.

That said, fresh food is far harder to tame. You're dealing with perishables, after all! So, if you want the best chance of success, you have to make sure that every new menu item is designed to meet all of your brand, financial, and operational criteria *before* you invest any resources into releasing it. And that demands a strategic framework.

In the chapters ahead, you are going to learn why brand fit is the golden thread you need to weave through every menu decision you make. I'll walk you through the steps you need to take to design your own annual food development calendar—and show you exactly why this cornerstone is so critical to any fresh food company. Finally, together, we'll dig into all the complex financial and operational mechanics that go so far beyond the cost of the ingredients in your cooler—and that matter so, so much in a world where margins are slim and facilities and teams can vary so widely. And at each point along the way I'll equip you with all the tools, templates, and actionable tips you need to set up, streamline, and perfect your own menu design strategy, along with the Mise Mode takeaways that will keep you on track and moving forward—always.

My hope is that, by the last page of this book, you'll have a solid understanding of all the moving parts in this process, along with the key strategies and tools you need to bring your recipe ideas and menus to market in a way that both delights *and* keeps you in business. If you can follow this playbook and use the customizable tools, you'll see that it's hard to go wrong. And, just maybe, you'll even contribute to solutions for a few of the food world's nagging problems along the way (food waste, wage parity... the list goes on). *It's all available to you.* Exciting, isn't it?

So let's get started!

Don't forget your free customizable menu planning tools before we get started!

1
KNOW YOUR MENU, KNOW THYSELF

Why It Always Comes Back to Your Brand

BRAND FIT COMES FIRST in this book because it needs to come first in your business—you absolutely cannot design a successful menu if you don't fully know your own brand. Understanding your brand's identity and purpose is fundamental to successful menu design—from the food product itself, to how you price it, to how you sell it to your customers. *Everything* flows from that understanding—absolutely *everything*. So, asking some critical questions and having alignment on the answers is always the first place to start.

The amount of investment that every major brand puts into understanding "who we are" is astronomical. And that's just the first step. From there, they dig into "what our customers think about us" and then "what our brand is saying to them." And on. And on. There are entire global agencies that specialize just in defining and fine-tuning the answers to these most basic questions. *Huge, huge money* is spent on this.

Because this is an R&D book and not a branding book, I'm going to keep these deets to a bare minimum—you can Google "define your brand agency" if you want the bigger picture. But I do want to give you an overview of what you need to think about in order to define and focus your brand.

Here, straight up, are the key brand attributes that every major brand drills into—and then locks down—to fully understand who they are.

Market and consumer research (a.k.a. consumer insights): This is where a company asks the right questions to the right people to learn who their customers are and what they care about. Are they affluent, or is money tight? Are they busy? Do they work long hours or do they have free time? How old are they? What is the gender split, if any? Are they single? Married? With kids? (Maybe they *are* kids?) How much does "healthier" matter to them? What is their understanding of what "healthier" means?

Visual identity: This is your brand's look and feel, from your logo to your corporate colors to your typeface and packaging.

Brand identity: This is your brand's mission, vision, and values—and how you show them to your customers.

Customer experience: This is your brand's voice and storytelling. It is also your typical consumer's experience at each point in their interaction with your brand, either online, handling your products, or ordering and eating it in your restaurant.

It's a lot to ask yourself! So if you're a small restaurant or a start-up brand that can't pony up major bucks to a big branding agency with a koi pond in their office, where do you begin? Without going too far down the rabbit hole, it's simple: ask yourself the same questions. Get your team together around the table, make a big pot of coffee (donuts optional), and start brainstorming your answers to questions like these:

- What is our brand concept in a few words?

- What is our personality? Who would we be if we were a person? *This is your avatar—a big part of your North Star to guide every development decision.*

- Why do customers come to us? What do they love? What *don't* they love? What do they expect from us? And then from there: Who is our ideal customer? What is *their* avatar? Some brands even give this ideal customer a name and refer to them directly when making decisions.

- What is our look, voice, and feel? What moods will a customer experience when they walk in or pick up one of our products?

- What are we signaling to the customer about how much they should expect to pay? (Think: the weight of your menu paper, the type of packaging, the quality of your cutlery—even if it's disposable. These details are all sending a message about your price point.)

- What is our mission? Our purpose? Our long-term aspirations? How do we accomplish our vision and hopes on the day-to-day? What are we trying to accomplish simply by existing?

- And, simply: What makes us unique?

Before you can decide what to create as a brand, you have to know who you are. If, for example, your mission is "to make delicious feel-good moments easy for everyone," then you know you need to make food items that are yummy, that evoke feelings of happiness and satisfaction, that are easy for folks to engage with, and that *really are* accessible and affordable to everyone. And it's about more than your products, too—it's about your whole *vibe*. And if you truly value that accessibility, the experience your customer navigates—from the moment they enter your doors or see your product on the shelf to the moment they're sweeping the crumbs away—has to be simple and seamless. That means a welcoming, non-intimidating space, friendly packaging, and plain language everywhere—no fancy talk here! Nothing complicated, just easy, delicious, feel-good moments. *That's McDonald's, by the way.*

Want to understand this further? Here's a useful exercise. The next time you walk into a restaurant, try *really* paying attention. Does it feel expensive or cheap? High energy or relaxed? Does it smell good, like fresh bread? Or sharp, like cleaning solution? Or does it not smell at all? Is it clean? Shiny? Bright? Muted? Is there loud music and a lot of chatter or is it calm and relaxed? Do the seats make you want to hang out for a while, or wolf your food and move on fast? Did you go up to get your sandwich or did a server come to your table? Everything in a restaurant environment adds up to one simple message that is communicated to every customer: "This is what you can expect here." The big brands are nailing this down, in every detail. And if you want to succeed in this world, you need to start thinking about those messages, too.

What Are Your Food Principles?

Part of knowing your brand means knowing what you want to represent through your plates—you know, the values that are informing your culinary principles. Have you ever wondered how decisions are made on which ingredients to purchase, or why a food maker will pick one ingredient over another? Large food brands rely on pre-determined food principles—"rules" that guide their purchasing and culinary teams and ensure brand integrity and consistency across every facet of their business.

How do you establish your food principles for your business? Answering these questions is a great place to start:

- Do you care about ingredient transparency? Organic certification?
- Do you care about local ingredients?
- Do you have requirements on environmental practices from your suppliers?
- Are there additives or chemicals in your food?
- Are your products manufactured or handmade?
- Do you have freshness standards for hot products? For baked goods? For beverages?
- What is your philosophy on culinary processes and techniques?
- Do you have seasonality and quality preferences for purchasing or handling? (For example, "tomatoes only when in season, sliced fresh and never refrigerated.")
- Do you have guidelines for who you purchase from? (For example, "We will purchase 30% of our ingredients from minority-owned businesses.")

Remember, these questions are only a guide, and a place to start. If you are just starting out, you might create answers to each of these questions that feel good to you, but find along the way that many of them are too cost prohibitive to practice fully. I mean, you might love to buy USDA certified organic, but can't afford to buy *everything* with that certification, so you buy it where it makes the most strategic sense and make incremental progress toward the goal you have set for your business. (Unless, that is, you are branding yourself as a fully organic brand, in which case you *have* to buy everything certified organic, all the time.)

Dietary Designation Matters, Too

This is an area that's becoming more important all the time. Menus that win offer a balanced selection, so it's important to create an intentional plan for how you want to design your menu in terms of meeting dietary preferences of a wide range of consumers.

Designations like vegan, vegetarian, diabetic, gluten-free, dairy-free, keto and more all have implications on a menu. From a commercial perspective, you would ideally be able to delight pretty much any customer who might walk in—or who might be making a choice for a group. (Think about it: if five people are deciding on a place to meet and only one is a vegetarian, *that's* the person who's going to have the biggest influence on where that group is eating their lunch.) So, think deeply about the range of options you want to have, how you can make tweaks to your recipes to ensure there are easy-to-find choices for a wide range of preferences, and, most importantly, *define* what those preferences mean to you and your business.

Take cheese as an example. Cheese is vegetarian, right? So can you simply mark a cheese sandwich as a veggie item on your menu and call it a day? Not so fast. A lot of cheese is made with animal rennet. What the heck is rennet? Well, traditionally, it's an ingredient sourced from the stomach lining of calves. So not, in fact, vegetarian after all. Okay, but what about eggs, then? Surely they're not meat—at least not yet. Not so fast again! A lot of vegetarians who are not necessarily vegan still do not eat eggs.

Doing your homework to ensure that your dietary designations are accurate and inclusive will help you avoid pitfalls like these. You may not be able to design *every* item to suit *every* consumer, but you will benefit by having *something* great on your menu for *any* consumer not just to find—but to find exciting. And the more variety in the options, the better. When they navigate your menu or your package labels—and especially when they question your staff members about your products—your customers need to be able to understand what exactly is in your food, and whether it's safe for them to eat. Building this kind of trust and clarity will go a long way toward creating a loyal fan base for your current menu and for any items you release in the future.

You Also Can't Forget About *Nutrition*

What goes into your food and onto your label is also about so much more than any one specific special diet. If you are serving food to people, you also have to remember that food, and everything in it, is the foundational energy that keeps us *all* healthy and alive. So when I am designing a menu item, nutrition is where I start.

Oh—and even if this isn't your own brand's #1 concern, there is also that not-so-small matter of labeling laws and nutrition guidelines. So go ahead and read this chapter anyway.

In my view, the first place to start when setting out your nutritional principles is to consider portion size. It's a tricky balance—as the average size of the portions that arrive on the typical American restaurant table swells over the edge of the plate, it's becoming harder and harder to maintain a healthy (in terms of body and profit) balance while still satisfying consumer expectations.

When I was running food development teams, I was often faced with pressure to build out larger portion sizes—think 16 ounces or more—and in response I would always say that a pound of food is a LOT to consume in one sitting. Like, a harmful amount. As a menu developer, you do have a responsibility not to put things out into the world that are going to harm people—at least that's how I see it. Appropriate portion sizes matter for many reasons: not just for health, but as a way to stem the outrageous food waste that is happening at every step of the supply chain, from the grower right to when the consumer dumps the rest of a too-large order into the trash. Once you set any expectations around portion size with your customers, it becomes part of your value proposition, and that is an extremely hard thing to change. So if you care about the impacts of "portion inflation," get it right from the outset and build your dishes for the right size at the right price.

You also have to think about what's going to appear on your label—as required by law, especially if you are selling food "to go." In the U.S., "to-go" labels must have precise calorie, ingredient, and allergen information once you reach a certain operational scale—but you may also want to offer your customers even more than that, to let them know that you know who they are and what they need. Before you even start testing a recipe, you need to set an acceptable content target range for things like calories, fat, saturated fat, and sugar. A lot of consumers will change their purchasing decision if they see nutritionals that exceed their own personal guidelines—but only sometimes. If I'm picking up lunch and the lentil veggie soup sounds awesome, but on closer inspection has twice the calories of the minestrone... on most days, I'm going to go with the minestrone. But not on every day. An ideal menu has a strategic balance of indulgent and health-based options, in order to capture both of those moods.

If your menu items have particular nutritional benefits, you may also want to highlight that: "an excellent source of X," for example, or "contains 80% of your required daily value of X," whether X is iron or fiber or folate or probiotics or vitamin C. If you aren't sure what nutritionals you are offering, get sure: just Google "nutrition calculation software" to find a ton of tools. Once you start building this step into your development process, you might be shocked by how quickly those calories add up. (Spoiler alert: dairy is the supreme calorie range buster *of all time*.)

How Many of Your Menu Items Consider Allergens?

An increasingly important element that you need to consider in your menu design is whether you are able to offer safety to people with food allergies. As a food provider, your personal responsibility in this area cannot be overstated.

There are so many common allergies out there, with impacts that span from a mild burning of the tongue to deadly asphyxiation. While a given individual might be looking at your food description to find evidence of allergens that range from lemons to garlic, the FDA lists nine categories of common allergies that you definitely need to be aware of:

- Milk (and all products with lactose)
- Fish (cod, bass, salmon)
- Shellfish (crab, shrimp, lobster)
- Tree nuts (almonds, walnuts, hazelnuts)
- Peanuts (yes, these are different from tree nuts)
- Wheat (that's your gluten)
- Soybeans (including the sauce—also often a source of gluten)
- Eggs (no explanation needed here, I think)
- Sesame (seeds and oil)

Again, arming your consumers with the knowledge they need to protect themselves comes down to providing options and clear labeling. Your label—and everyone who serves your food onsite—should be able to lay out exactly what's in that product—right down to your cooking spray, the ingredients in your spice blend, and even the foods that share a kitchen with what you're serving. If you need a real-life example for your teams, try this one: If a customer wants the BBQ chicken pizza but says they are allergic to alliums, can you serve it to them? *Garlic, onions, chives, scallions, and leeks are all alliums. And, yes, some folks are deeply allergic to them.* You and your team would need to be able to say with 100% accuracy that yes, there are red onions in the pizza toppings and garlic and onions in the BBQ sauce, so they should pick a different pizza. Or what about a customer who is allergic to eggs? That means cooked egg, too. So, your team needs to know that your frosted lemon shortbread cookie uses meringue powder in the glaze (hello, egg whites!), and the tagliatelle in your pasta Bolognese has egg in it as well (yep, lots of pastas have egg). This is the level of information—on every product you serve—that has to be a) immediately available and b) absolutely accurate, so that your teams can respond with confidence to any ingredient or preparation question asked of them. That's the only way you can ensure the health and safety of your customers.

The Delight Factor

It's not all serious—or at least it shouldn't be. One of the greatest philosophies I learned over all my years running development teams in high-volume environments was this: Don't be afraid to have FUN! I am officially giving you full permission to put things on your menu that won't sell a ton, but will send amazing signals to your customers about who you are as a brand and what you care about.

Let's say you want to persuade your customers to reduce their meat consumption, even though your core menu is heavy with animal proteins. Sure, add some vegan salads and baked goods to your menu—but don't call them out as "vegan" with a bunch of big labels. Trust me, the actual vegans who come into your stores will be looking for those products, and will be delighted to spot them. But your existing customer base—who come to you looking for what they expect to find—doesn't need to be whacked over the head with that word. For them, create some menu copy that describes the item in fun, unignorable ways, perhaps using the fact that it's vegan as a "condiment on the side" rather than the headline. Think: "triple chocolate indulgence muffin" with a tiny "vegan" label on it rather than "vegan chocolate muffin."

One time, I put a sandwich stuffed with super clean-ingredient potato chips on a national menu—not because I thought it would sell a ton, but because it sent a signal that we were an approachable, fun, and delightful place to find delicious and nostalgic products. (At least nostalgic for anyone who used to do this when they were a kid.) All of this to say: use your menu to send signals that reinforce your brand values and food principles. Your customers will enjoy those unique items, and it will create opportunities for you to put your values into action.

That's a Brand Wrap

You might be wondering by now why we've gone down such a long road about what goes into your food when we're still talking about your brand. Again, it comes down to two things: your food principles and your relationship with your customer. You need to know who you are, what you are serving, and why. And your customer needs to know those exact same things.

Once you have alignment on your identity and your food principles, they can act as your beacon whenever you are facing a difficult choice or feeling lost at any point in the menu design process. These brand guidelines should not just be a thing that lives in your head. They should be a fluid, living document that you share and update on an ongoing basis as your brand evolves, menu expands, and trends, laws and regulations, and your overall nutritional goals change.

IT'S TIME TO GET INTO MISE MODE

Before you even set a frying pan on a stove to test out a new menu item idea, you need to get your brand in order. That means doing the work.

1. Get to understand who you are as a brand. What makes you unique? What matters to you? What are your food principles? That is your guiding light when designing your new menu.

2. As important as knowing yourself is, so is knowing your customer. Actually think about who they would be as a person, then create a customer avatar to represent them. Keep that person in mind with every decision you make.

3. Educate yourself and your team about nutrition, allergens, and labeling, and making sure your customers know what they're about to eat—and can trust that it's safe for them.

Did you grab your downloadable tools yet?

2

KEEP THAT MENU WHEEL TURNING

How to Create an Annual Development Calendar

NOTHING IS DONE on a whim at the world's most successful food companies. There is no universe in which a major food brand is resting on the shoulders of a lone chef who designs each menu by throwing together off-the-cuff dishes in a kitchen somewhere. Instead, it takes decision after decision in department after department, all based on the business metrics and factors that drive each team's particular sphere of expertise—whether that's costing, purchasing, training, packaging, marketing, or sales. But here's the good news: if you're among the 70% of U.S. restaurants that are independently owned and operated and you don't *have* the gift of multiple teams of experts working alongside you, you can still borrow from the same processes and strategies that underpin the success of the big brands. And it all starts with making sure that your menu stays exciting and fresh.

See, as humans, we have short attention spans. When you walk into your usual spot to pick up some lunch, you want to see something new on the menu as often as possible—and if you don't, you start to get bored. *Tuscan chicken wrap? I already ate that earlier this week. Tabouleh bowl? That was okay in the summer but now I want something hearty. Baked potato chowder? Again? No thanks.*

This consumer tendency makes "Limited Time Only" your new best friend. Continuously igniting a sense of excitement and surprise through a constant cycle of seasonal innovation is what will keep your food brand interesting and top-of-mind for your customers. Using specials as the vehicle for testing while keeping your core menu solid and stable is the "sweet spot." But! There are some customers who really just like to enjoy the same grilled chicken mozzarella pesto sandwich every time they stop in. They fall in love, they know what to expect, and they want it on the menu—looking, tasting, and costing the same as always. (There is a reason why franchise food businesses are big businesses.) You need to serve both customer behaviors with your menu—and the best way to do that while keeping your core customer base happy is leaning on your seasonal specials to test and tweak. Some of your new products may hit that proverbial spot and find a place on your permanent menu. Some may work only as a recurring special. And some may need to be parked in the land of "never again."

This strategic turnover (is that a food pun?) is just the largest gear in a very complex piece of machinery. Because so many parts of your operation will be affected by each product development decision—and, if you work in a large organization, so many various executives and managers will want to weigh in and sign off on those decisions—it is critical that you alert and align all of these stakeholders to "what's coming down the pike." And that's why you need—really *need*—an annual food development calendar. It's not just a planning tool—it's a communications tool. And if you're an independent owner or operator? Even better. You can run your menu systems in the same way the larger, better-resourced companies do, and profit from the cycles and structure these strategies provide. I'm about to walk you through how to make yours—to follow along, use the QR codes throughout this book to get your own customizable templates, along with bonus tutorials on how to get the most out of them.

Step 1: Organize Your Menu into Categories

Who doesn't love spreadsheets! Oh, is that just me? Well, learn to love them, because they're the easiest way to take all the food-y and beverage-y bits and pieces on your menu and turn them into a cohesive system.

You need to have a real-time view of your menu and all of its moving parts if you want to make good decisions about what you should be selling, how you should be pricing it, and where you should be focusing your resources. So, to get started, make a list of every single item that you're currently selling—from the drip coffee to the chocolate cake—and organize it into food and drink categories, like:

- Hot Entrées
- Salads
- Grain Bowls (Hot & Cold)
- Tacos/Pizzas
- Sandwiches (Hot & Cold)
- Soups (Hot & Cold)
- Desserts
- Snacks
- Drinks (Hot & Cold)
- Countertop Items
- To Go/Takeaway-only Products
- Retail Food Products

And any other category that makes sense for your business. That's the first column of your spreadsheet. Next to that, make a column that lists every menu item you have, placing them within the appropriate category. So, by "Salads," you'd have:

- Chicken Caesar Salad
- Salmon Caesar Salad
- Classic Caesar Salad
- Spicy Taco Salad
- Summer Bean Salad

And so on. The key is to capture every item—and to use the exact same names and language that you use on your menu and your sales points.

Then, next to that create more columns to write in more details on each item:

- Date of introduction
- Current sales price
- Dietary notes
- Allergens
- Any other factors that are relevant to your business

Now you have an accurate view of what you're selling. Your next task is to plan out when you're going to sell it.

Step 2: List Out Your Annual Landmarks

Here's a trade secret of the food business: the team that designed that pumpkin spice latte you like to enjoy in September did not start planning its release in August. If you want to offer seasonal and holiday food items (and I recommend that you do), you need to plan those puppies ahead. Far ahead.

Why? Because it takes a long time to get a good marketing campaign into gear. (And that's aside from all the purchasing, packaging, and training considerations.) So if everyone in your organization can see the long view on what they need to prepare for, it makes it that much easier to get each department to agree to your amazing ideas.

Let's just say it like it is: getting that buy-in is another reason why seasons and holidays are your friend. From the management perspective, whatever your department, it's way more comfortable to agree to seasonal product development opportunities than it is to green-light a permanent investment, upgrade, or menu change. *Special Valentine's dessert for two? We love it! Start buying our sliced cheddar from a higher-quality producer? Um . . . do we have to? Let's discuss that later.*

You see what I mean.

And if you are an independent restaurant owner or operator, starting with your annual calendar will keep you organized and on track, just like your larger competitors are.

So, get yourself another spreadsheet (or get the template from the nearest QR code!), and start listing out every holiday, event, and seasonal period that might in any way be relevant to your business or meaningful to your customers. Your list might look like this:

January 1	New Year's Day	July 4	Independence Day
February 14	Valentine's Day	September 21	First day of fall
March 21	First day of spring	October 31	Halloween
April 8	Easter	November 22	Thanksgiving
May 13	Mother's Day	December	Christmas/Hannukah
June 17	Father's Day	December 21	First day of winter
June 22	First day of summer		

You might also want to consider local events (New York Cider Week?), school holidays (spring break!), special interest events (Earth Day?), community and religious holidays, and anything else that might be a touchpoint for your customers. These are now the spokes in your annual development calendar—something to plan your menu around not weeks ahead, but *a full year* ahead.

There are tons of options for how you might want to take advantage of these events and holidays. Most major fresh food chains follow a cycle that looks like this:

Quarterly specials: Products that run for about 3 months.

Monthly specials: These change every 4 weeks.

Seasonal specials: Limited-time offers that typically last about 1 to 3 weeks, often tied to a holiday (green milkshakes! heart-shaped pastries! summer coolers!).

Look for opportunities to really create a sense of *newness* for your customers. Keep each category on your list fresh and exciting, and use each temporary product as a testing opportunity to learn more about what your customers want. These cyclical menus are brilliant for fine-tuning your financials, so use them as strategically as you can.

Oh, and here's a fun restaurant industry fact: Did you know that Mother's Day is the biggest sales day of the year?

Step 3: Build Out Your Complete Plan

Now it's time to identify the immediate and longer-term culinary and business priorities that you want to build into your annual development calendar. (Yes, your business priorities are part of your menu planning, too!)

Your priorities are going to look different depending on your business, but list out the twelve months ahead, divide them into quarters, and then consider what you want to accomplish in each of the four quarters ahead—from the near-term to the end of the year—along with their ideal launch dates. This calendar might include things like:

- Brand-new menu features you want to launch
- Those special seasonal products
- Switching any food items from outside vendors to in-house (for example, making your own ketchup or iced tea)
- New product lineups or categories (like introducing new hot grain bowls)
- Behind-the-scenes menu changes (like changing up an ingredient, or the vendor you get it from)

Here's a template version of my Mise Mode annual development calendar to give you an idea of what this looks like:

Mise Mode Annual Development Calendar

Buckets	Q1	Q2	Q3	Q4
Product Development: Existing Category				
New Batch Recipe Development & Ingredient Upgrades				
New Categories & Test Projects				
Continuous Team Training				
Launch Dates				

You'll notice that this is also an ideal place to include continuous or one-off team trainings like food or workplace safety sessions—remember, these necessary programs are competing for your team's resources, time, and attention just like everything else, so you need to prioritize and plan to make sure they happen. And heck, while you're at it, why not expand yours to include what your competitors typically do in each quarter, what larger food trends are happening locally and around the globe in the months ahead, and even the insights you're gleaning from your own sales data about what needs to be tweaked, updated, or swapped out? Information is power, and this is power, baby!

(Psst... want to skip the work of creating your menu development calendar from scratch? You guessed it—jump to your nearest QR code for a free downloadable Mise Mode template.)

So, I bet you're looking at all of these projects, menu upgrades, product launches, business priorities, future trends, and special holidays and thinking that your year is looking *very, very* jam-packed. Well, that's all stuff that you were going to have to do—or try to do—anyway. Now you're just aware of it, and in a position to prepare for it, communicate it, and move forward with it in the most strategic possible way. Can you see now how important it is to keep *all* of these moving parts under one umbrella?

If you don't take the long and wide view on what's ahead, any one of those wheels in motion could sweep down like a surprise and upend all of your amazing menu ideas before they've even had a chance to see daylight. Making sure that anyone who could potentially have a say in the matter, whose need for resources intersects with yours, or who has a role to play in ensuring that your plans go smoothly (hello, finance, procurement, HR, marketing, operations, etc.) is prepared, on board, and ready to "sign off" will help you avoid time-wasting pitfalls like "why are you rolling out new mozzarella grilled cheese when what we really need are more desserts," or "why are we introducing toasted sandwiches when we need to redo our baguette sandwich lineup," or whatever question might land in front of you too late in the game if folks don't know what you're up to and why. Building and sharing an annual calendar will create full visibility across your business and give every department the ability to play their part successfully. (And, if you are an independent owner or operator and all of these "teams" are *you*, the same applies in terms of considering the implications of all of these different business areas so you aren't spending all of your future time on putting out fires and untangling conflicting priorities.)

IT'S TIME TO GET INTO MISE MODE

If you don't plan ahead, you're going to end up spending most of your time, energy, and resources trying to get a handle on the same events that seem to surprise you every year. Get ahead of the game with a menu development calendar.

1. List and categorize all of the menu items you already sell so you can look for gaps, dead weight, and opportunities.

2. Identify every holiday, local event, and seasonal theme you want to take advantage of, along with all of the other business priorities across your organization that will need time and resources in the year ahead.

3. Use what you've learned to build out your annual development calendar, making sure to get buy-in from every team member, manager, and executive who has a say or whose work intersects with those plans.

It's true! All of these QR codes lead to the same awesome kit of tools and tutorials.

3

"CALORIES IN, CALORIES OUT"

It's Time to Look at the Money Side

WHEN IT COMES TO DEVELOPING any menu item—never mind an entire annual menu strategy—it's critical to understand the financial targets and goals of your business, along with any operational constraints that might affect what you are capable of producing. You basically need to know what success looks like so you can "back into" it. You don't want to invest anything into developing a product that your customers won't pay for, that your chefs can't replicate exactly across every kitchen you operate, or—and this happens a lot—that costs so much to produce and distribute that it won't deliver enough profit to support your business. So, looking closely at your targets and holding them up as a guiding light is a fundamental practice.

Readers of *A Taste of Opportunity* may remember a catchy little saying I used in my own operations to explain the money side of food to my teams: "Calories in versus calories out." Everyone knows that if you want to maintain a particular weight, you have to balance the calories you take in through food with the calories you expend through movement and exercise. Let that formula get out of balance and your weight is going to change, one way or the other.

The same formula applies to business. Your revenue (calories in) has to *at least* match your costs (calories out) if you want your doors to stay open. And that doesn't even touch on profit. Let me remind you: there is only one way a food company can make money, and that's through selling food and drink—*at enough of a profit to pay for the cost of running your business*. Plus more, if you can swing it.

So, if your recipes aren't built for deliciousness, craveability, *and* profit, then you and everyone on your team are screwed. I mean, just think about what else has to get paid out after you have factored in the ingredient costs. The profit from your recipes has to cover rent, utilities, equipment, repairs, maintenance, insurance, licensing, point-of-sale equipment, marketing, theft (yup) and breakage, accounting and bookkeeping, cleaning, furniture, linens, packaging, dishes and glasses, and all those gorgeous cooking implements. And then there are your employees! (You know—all that labor to actually make the things you make and sell the things you sell?) There are salaries, of course, but then there are also training programs, recruitment costs, HR services, payroll companies, and benefits. And don't get me started on all the "unknown unknowns" that we all come up against in the food business. And if I haven't said it enough, the only thing paying for all of this is all of that wonderful food and drink that you put on your menu.

Literally your *whole business* is dependent on the profit that you build into what you sell. So you better be damn sure that you a) know what your financial goals are, and b) are able to hit them. There is no way around this—what you sell has to make money. Okay sure, there are a couple of exceptions to this rule, including "loss leaders" (which are basically "strategically enticing" menu items that are priced low enough to get customers in the door—profit be damned—on the assumption, or at least the hope, that they'll buy a few of the more profitable items while they're there). But while strategies like this can sometimes be effective, they can tank your financials if you aren't keeping a close eye. They are a dangerous game—while planning for solid profits will never let you down.

What's Your Competition Up To?

One of the biggest areas of impact when it comes to ensuring your financials are on target is looking outside of your business. I know, right? Sounds weird to be told to not focus solely on your own operation. But here's the thing: just like you have to know who you are from a brand perspective to guide your menu development decisions, it's equally important to know what's already available to your customers from your closest competitors. Whether it's comparing pricing, menu offerings, quality, or marketing campaigns, you can't outsmart the other businesses if you haven't done a competitive review.

Take oatmeal. (Yes, oatmeal.) Let's say you are considering adding this hearty hot breakfast item to your menu. Where else could your customers get it? How are other businesses serving it? What is the price range? And don't just look at businesses in your own exact market—get the whole picture. Make a list of oatmeal offerings from your five closest competitors across niches like indie restaurants, coffee shops, breakfast joints, and national chains, or even hotels. Then, have a look online or in real life and gather intel on each, paying attention to all of the details that follow (and yes, an example and Mise Mode template is available in the downloadable tool package linked throughout this book!):

- Description copy (including ingredients)
- Portion size
- Packaging
- Sales price
- Flavor options
- Speed of service
- Quality
- Any other special notes

All of this information will tell you what customers in various markets are expecting from a price, quality, and convenience standpoint—and it will also give you the full view of where the opportunity lies in the marketplace for your own badass oatmeal. Do you want to offer the lowest price? Or the highest-quality product, with expensive added touches like whole almonds and mixed berry compote? To-go or dine in? Oh hey, is everyone else serving theirs with dairy? That sounds like a gap in the market for vegans that you could fill with a side of oat milk. It's all about seeing what's already available so you can offer something unique, and uniquely *you*. If you just repeat someone else's offer—same quality, price, flavor, convenience—and don't bring your own value to the market, your oatmeal will likely land with a thud.

Let's Talk Profit

Now that you know what your competition is doing, it's time to roll up your sleeves and get to work on building your menu product for optimal financial performance.

For the purposes of this exercise (setting aside inflation, supply chain issues, and all the other fun stuff of the modern era), let's set a simple target of 25% for food items—that's the goal we are going to reverse engineer our product into. It's really important to set a specific goal for all of your development so that you don't waste time building recipes that will never provide the margins you need to actually keep running your business, lest you find yourself literally paying your customers to eat your food. *I have seen this happen. A lot!* A chef-owner creates a dish that is beloved by patrons and sells like, well, hotcakes—and it ends up destroying the financial health of the business. Don't let that be you—take your time and build this plan out properly. Discipline matters.

Weighted Averages, Baby!

I don't want to spend too much time on weighted averages, but this is an important touchpoint to explore with your team if you have the resources. Each category you have on your menu should have a different targeted "cost of goods sold" percentage—or COGS%, for those in the know. If you have a quick Google, you'll see that different categories have a different expected COGS range—say, 10% for beverages, or 30% for desserts, or 26% for salads. The overall sum of those COGS percentages is your weighted average.

One of the biggest gifts you can give your business is to secure a financial wizard for your team who can do tons of projections and modeling to help you understand how different financial scenarios will play out against each other.

- What happens when you take all these different categories and their different potential for profit and put them all together?
- How can you drive more sales of the most profitable items?

- What doesn't make much profit but brings in customers who buy other things?
- How close can you get to that 25% goal when all the different categories on your menu are put together and everything is considered?

And have you factored in ingredient yields—meaning the less-than-you-think share of the ingredients you buy that you can actually use and sell? (By the way, this step is so, so, so, so critical—*do not* ignore those food waste costs when you are doing your costing projections. Apple cores weigh more than you think, and some foods spoil fast.)

I'm telling you, turning all these various dials up and down and projecting the effects is seriously fun stuff. Sit down with your best finance person and see for yourself.

So, What Does that Sandwich Actually Cost?

Your COGS% may give you a rough idea of what a particular menu item is going to cost based on its category, but you won't really know until you drill down into that salad bowl, or that donut, or that avocado-and-ricotta-cheese sandwich and actually build out the recipe—including a placeholder sales price. So that means it's time to pull out another spreadsheet. Hooray!

To build your recipe cost calculator for each of your proposed menu items (or—and you can probably see this coming—to skip the building part, just jump on one of those QR codes for the Mise Mode template link), you need to list out each individual ingredient that goes into each recipe—right down to the salt and pepper—and the specific amount of it in each serving (by gram, or by piece, or whatever unit is appropriate for the ingredient). Then, multiply those together to get the price for each ingredient for every individual sale of that item. *This is the place where those pesky ingredient yields really matter—so (seriously!) make sure those are factored into your costs.* At the bottom, add up that final column to get your total cost per menu item, and divide it by your sales price—that's your COGS%. Here's how this might look:

Mise Mode Recipe Cost Calculator

Category: Sandwich–HOT
Recipe Name: Signature Grilled Cheese

Ingredient	Amount	Unit	Cost
Bread–Sourdough Wheat	2	each	0.43
Roasted Garlic & Basil Aioli	40	g	0.32
Cheese–Jarlsberg, Sliced	56	g	0.38
Cheese–Gruyère, Sliced	56	g	0.45
Cheese–Parmesan	28	g	0.28
Seasoning Mix	1	g	0.015

Total Cost	$1.88
Sales Price	$7.19
COGS%	26%
Profit/Contribution	$5.32
LIVE/Intro Date	11.1.23

Now you know the actual dollar-value profit you are going to be making off each sale of that menu item (based on food cost alone—we're leaving staff, overhead, packaging, and all those other little details off the table for now). How is it looking? Is it viable? When it's all totaled up, is that final COGS going to move you closer toward your 25% goal when you look at your weighted averages? If not, what could you adjust in that list of costs and tweak the recipe to make it work?

As you dream up new products (ones that are always in line with your food principles and nutritional goals!), you are going to find yourself spending a good chunk of time weighing, adjusting, and reconsidering recipes in an effort to make your culinary dreams actually work from a financial perspective. I mean, it's really easy to design a delicious dish. It's way harder to design a dish that will make enough profit to support your business. This is the place to be *ruthless* with discipline—all in service to the sustainability of your business.

Don't Forget to Factor in Customer Trust

Here's something I see happen all the time, and it just breaks my heart: a food business releases an excellent product that customers love, but they don't do the work ahead of time to make sure it's a financial winner. So *after* the customers have come to rely on that product, the management team starts making the decision to raise the price and reduce the quality, bit by bit. A cheaper cheese here, less mustard there, swapping out romaine for iceberg... all while crossing their fingers and hoping no one notices. Believe me, they notice. Your customers can become very attached to the experience that you have consistently been delivering to them. Sure, you can make small tweaks and cuts to products here are and there if and when you need to—but you have to tread carefully. Make a small change, then watch, wait, and listen—and reverse course when you need to. Your customers trust you, and that trust is a precious and fragile thing.

Yes, you will face a lot of pressure to make changes to your menu items in support of a better financial outcome—now more than ever. (Food prices! I know!!) I speak from experience—I've made many menu decisions that I did not feel happy about but had to execute to meet company targets. It happens. The only thing you can do in moments like these is invest the time and effort into figuring out your best path forward to balance a dependable customer experience with the bottom line. (Here's an insider tip: Often, it's far more productive—and more profitable—to drop a nonviable menu item altogether and start fresh with something new.) It's a tightrope, but if you have a popular product that isn't working on the financial side, you're going to have to walk it.

Of course, you've already guessed what your Plan A should be: avoid the tightrope altogether and develop a profitable product before the first customer ever tastes it. Now that's a winning formula.

IT'S TIME TO GET INTO MISE MODE

Your menu decisions are the lifeblood of your food business—they are literally going to decide whether or not you make money. Putting financial goals at the heart of the development of each menu item will keep you in the black.

1. Identify your COGS% for each of your categories, and your overall weighted-average COGS% target.

2. Build out your master recipe template—remembering (always!) to include considerations like ingredient yield and packaging. Even if you don't offer portable grab-and-go items, what about doggie bags or delivery? Make sure you plan for every single product and every single penny.

3. Adjust each recipe as needed until it's absolutely delicious *and* a financial winner. And once you release it and your customers love it, be sure to protect that trust.

Don't miss out on these customizable menu planning templates!

4

LET'S PLAY OPERATIONS

How to Get Your Whole Team in Lock Step

BY NOW YOU'RE STARTING to understand that you can't separate your great menu ideas from the other teams that contribute to your organization, whether that's the marketing folks who have to create and design the ads and table signs, the finance team who can help you figure out your weighted COGS% projections, the procurement team and vendors who have to find the ingredients you need at a price you can afford, the operators who have to figure out how to efficiently get those products into people's hands, and right down to the servers who need to know every detail about those products so when a customer asks "what kind of meat is pastrami made out of?" they'll know how to answer.

If you're feeling overwhelmed (and, again, if all of those teams put together amount to just you because you're an owner or operator who does mostly everything, you probably are feeling overwhelmed), take heart: while all of these interconnected operations can be tough to manage, there are plenty of handy tools to help you out. Beginning with my favorite product launch organizer—the Mise Mode Launch Timeline.

The Mise Mode Launch Timeline is a simple template I adopted from a product launch management process created by one of my favorite food and beverage mentors: Matt Delaney, a head operations advisor at Mise Mode and someone who worked his way from dishwasher and busser to $200-million COO. This template has successfully shepherded many food launches over the years, across many different multi-million-dollar food brands. It follows a fundamental principle that was taught to me early on and has since proven to be one of the most important lessons I have ever been given: *keep things simple*.

This timeline—which, of course, is (say it with me) downloadable with the Mise Mode tool package you'll find linked with every QR code throughout this book—counts down the development of a menu item from 13 weeks out to the launch date. It's designed to help you keep all those crazy moving parts in sync and on schedule: meetings, calculations, sign offs, communications, operations and equipment, testing, purchasing, labeling, training—all the way to "go time." It captures every person and team involved, each stakeholder who needs to be on board, and each step needed along the way to keep everyone informed and on track. This is a very complex spreadsheet, and I am not even going to *try* to reproduce it within the confines of this book (so download it! quick!), but here is the gist. Your key columns will include:

Action items: Top-line tasks include team meetings, recipe development, testing, purchasing, pricing, developing nutritionals, equipment considerations, training materials and development, packaging and print material development and production, IT considerations, marketing/advertising planning, restaurant setup, distribution, stocking, and more.

Completion target dates: Starting from 13 weeks out and including all top-line items plus subcategory actions like specific training meetings or having print materials laminated and on display.

Team responsible: Purchasing, marketing, training, your food teams, and so on.

Task status: A live field where you keep track of what's done, what's pending, and what's underway.

Completed date: Self-obvious, but I will say that it feels great to mark this one in.

Take your Mise Mode template, customize the list, slot in the dates, and boom—you have a rock-solid plan to ensure a smooth launch, with nothing being left to chance. And if you are an independent owner or operator? Same process for you, too—except instead of being surrounded by departments, you likely have a combination of talented folks and vendors who can support your launch efforts. Just customize this timeline to your unique needs of your business, and you're ready to go!

Now that you have a picture of a complete timeline where you can see all the moving parts in one place, let's take a deeper look into each of the departments (or areas of focus, if you're a skeleton crew) that need to come to the table to support a successful launch.

Your Marketing Team

Marketing matters a ton when it comes to ensuring a successful launch. Whether you have a team of dedicated marketing and communications experts or one solo staff member with a talent for creating punchy social media posts, this is one area that you can't ignore when it comes to creating the right impact on your customers and their experience with your new product.

The list of what this team could be working to produce is endless: physical print material for your stores (think holiday window displays, table toppers, napkins...), the language you use on your menu, product labels, in-house marketing materials (table toppers or printed napkins, etc.), social media campaigns, visual app updates, giveaways—even just the right words to write in chalk on your sidewalk sandwich board. All of that work needs time to ideate, plan, and execute, so you have to bring whoever is responsible for this area of business into the conversation right from the beginning. The minute you know exactly what the items are that you're going to put on an upcoming menu, *that's* when you need to be connecting with this team so that they can get to work and have everything ready for launch date.

Your Purchasing Team

In the same way that you don't want to get fixated on pet recipes that will never fill those three buckets of menu design success—a.k.a. your financial, operational, and nutritional targets—you also don't want to invest valuable time into making products that require ingredients that you won't be able to acquire in sufficient or consistent amounts.

The global food supply chain has always been a mysterious, temperamental, and many-tentacled beast—and I am speaking as a one-time ingredient broker, so trust me, I know—but with climate impacts, political instability, labor shortages, that wild food-price inflation I mentioned earlier, and all the complexities of our wacky modern world, that beast is more ornery and unpredictable than ever. And that's *on top* of everything you already have to consider as a food developer, like ingredient seasonality and availability, package size, logistics, shelf life, storage considerations (i.e., how much space you actually have in your walk-in, freezer, and shelves), temperature requirements, special handling needs, import issues... and so much more.

This all becomes especially complicated when your brand has firm rules in place for ingredient integrity. (Remember those food principles from chapter 1? Highest available quality? Hyperlocal? Organic? Minimal packaging? From-scratch cooking? Fair labor practices? Whatever your brand values are, you won't be doing yourself a favor by abandoning them when things get tough.)

Once you've nailed down your recipe and you know how much of each ingredient you need, your purchasing team (or person, or just you) will need plenty of time to line up that supply chain, ensure the right ingredient provenance based on your food principles, and confirm the final pricing (as much as possible, anyway) with your vendors. And not just your ingredients—all of those nice things your marketing team is working on also need materials and vendor relationships. Purchasing teams are busy all the time! And frankly, they are core to every business's financial success—in *A Taste of Opportunity* I called them the "Meryl Streep" of the food industry for their versatility and ability to generate financial success, and I would still give them all the Oscars today. You absolutely need every ounce of their negotiation, analytical, and project management skills if you want that new menu to generate a profit, so always keep them in the loop. *Hot tip:* Sometimes your purchasing team will bring fun, exciting new products to you! Vendors share new items all the time—gorgeous first cold-press olive oil tapenade, truly sun-dried tomatoes ready to make your salad dreams come true... let them know that you're open and curious and you will love some of the products that make their way to you.

Your IT and Finance Teams

The days of cash registers and server notepads are loooong gone. So when you are updating that menu, you also need to get your point-of-sale software, order management systems, digital menu boards, and inventory tracking apps updated, too. Like with all things, the devil is in the details, and it's going to take time to update those systems, ensure the correct pricing is connected to the correct products, remove the old ingredients and products and add the new ones, and generally get it all accurate, double-checked, and ready to execute. Pulling your IT and finance teams in early in the process, connecting them with each other, and ensuring they both have time to work through any hiccups is critical as you make your way toward that launch. You'd be surprised by how many moving parts there are between all of the various software systems in a modern food operation—especially when online and app-based ordering is involved—and the impact those fine details can have on the financial reporting side of your business. And yes: any hiccups that arise because your IT and finance teams were not up to speed with everyone else can and will create distraction (at best) or true chaos (at worst) on launch day. So use your Mise Mode Launch Timeline! Seriously!

Your Kitchen and Guest-facing Teams

Your kitchen team is the obvious and critical place to focus on when bringing your menu strategy to life. Everything from their individual roles and skills, the speed of their service targets, the consistent execution of the recipes, and the training wrapped around all of it should be front and center as you solidify your development plans. And it's the same for your guest-facing teams. I can't stress enough how important it is to include the guest-facing team members who will actually be selling and serving your new menu items—and leaving their mark on your customers as they do it—in your launch process. You could build the most delicious, nutritious, profitable, well-packaged, and perfectly marketed little chopped-egg salad bowl into your offerings, and if your front-line staff don't know what kind of lettuce it uses, whether there is bacon in it, how to apply the dressing, or if the nuts are mixed in or served on the side, you're going to hit a very hard wall. *So hello, team training—it's fun to see you here!*

Your best friend in terms of consistent and efficient execution of your new menu item is a little one-pager called a job aide. These handy "kitchen recipes" pair step-by-step instructions with photos and tips to help everyone in your kitchens prepare a product accurately. You can list out the weight of each ingredient, how to execute with the right portioning tools, the correct timing and order of steps, how to store it, and what it should look like when it's completed.

Mise Mode Job Aide Template

Recipe Name: Grilled Lamb Lollipops
Recipe Date: 11.1.23
Category: Meat, Entrée

Ingredient	Quantity	Unit
Lamb Chops	3	each
Pork Fat (Lard)	1	tbsp
Maldon Sea Salt	1/8	tsp
Black Pepper	1/8	tsp

Method

1 Melt the lard in a saucepot until liquid in consistency.

2 Dip the lamb chops in the melted lard and fully coat the meat (all sides).

3 Rest chops between sheets of parchment paper and hold in fridge until ordered (fully sealed in plastic wrap).

To Finish:

4 Preheat your grill to med-high temp.

5 Once grill is hot, add chops and grill for 1 minute, then flip to other side for 1 minute.

6 Flip back and cook between 15-30 seconds depending on the thickness of your chop. Should be medium rare.

7 Serve immediately with pinch of Maldon, black pepper, and lemon wedges.

Special Notes: Should be served medium rare unless guest requests differently. Contains pork and lamb.

Create one for each product, have a team use it to make sure it's clear, and then have an easily accessed place to keep laminated versions in every kitchen. (Get started with making your own by grabbing! the Mise Mode templates! linked throughout this book!)

Don't forget to consult your top kitchen team members during recipe development, too. Getting their insight on best practices for how to streamline execution and on the prep required to make each item will 100% translate to improved financial performance. *Another hot tip:* The fewer ingredients and the less amount of human-hand work you need to bring a recipe to life, the less you will spend on labor, the less room there will be for error, and the less food waste will end up in your compost bins. There's big money in simplification—and working with your kitchen team for additional ways to optimize can help you find it.

And here's something that seems obvious but is more rarely practiced than you'd think: the best way to ensure accurate execution of your menu items is to actually *talk* to your teams. I'm not just talking about a list of instructions or steps, or arming them with a few catchy sales descriptions. I'm talking about helping your team understand *why* each decision was made. Why a customer's experience needs to be consistent every time they purchase the product. Why the cold storage needs to be so cold. Why the bread is toasted for exactly two minutes, or why the five-bean chili is held at 140°F. *All* of the whys—or as much as you can deliver. The more you can connect the dots for your teams, the better your customer experience will be, and the more money you will make.

Take portioning. When one of your kitchen team members over-portions the tuna salad on a sandwich by using the wrong sized portioning tool (or skips the tool altogether), they're likely thinking, *What's the big deal? Plus, it will make the customer happy, cuz bigger = better, so it's a good thing, right?* A totally understandable thought if you don't have access to the big picture! It's a game changer if you can show your team members that picture by adding context to your training and helping them understand that the actual profits on that sandwich are miniscule—and it's that razor-thin margin that's paying for the wage deposits that land in their bank account every two weeks (not to mention the free snacks in the staff room). And you can also help them understand that while a customer might be pleased with an overstuffed sandwich on one visit, they're going to be pissed on their next visit when they get the real portion from a different staff member who is executing the recipe accurately. *A trusting customer relationship broken, for a half-ounce of tuna.* You have the opportunity to solve this problem before it happens—by building out a proper, well-thought-out training plan that includes the "whys" and slotting it into your Mise Mode Launch Timeline.

You Can't Schedule Inspiration—But You Can Plan for It

While the Mise Mode Launch Timeline is an amazing tool for keeping your product launch on track, it only begins when you have already done the hard work of identifying the products, categories, and recipes you need to develop. On top of all the menu analysis and calendar work you started doing in chapters 2 and 3, you should also be having weekly conversations with your colleagues and team members about any new ideas or areas of opportunity that might have cropped up—not necessarily to cram into your calendar right now, but to put on the back burner (to use a kitchen metaphor so obvious I can hardly bear to type it). In my world, I call this "the parking lot," and it's a valuable source for solutions and inspiration that will always be there on standby, waiting for you to dig into.

To make sure you are capturing all of the menu-development energy and potential that exists across your organization, make sure you plan in regular, unscripted time to check in with each team:

Purchasing: These folks have access to the vendors and suppliers who are always sharing new ingredients and products. They also see big price increases ahead, ensure supply chain and logistics are factored in, and can negotiate relationships and volume contracts to mitigate pricing fluctuations.

Kitchen and guest-facing teams: This one is a gimme when it comes to menu ideas. Make sure they know you want to hear those ideas (both theirs, and the ones they hear from your customers)—often, people need an invite to know their input is welcome and will be heard.

IT/finance: Your finance teams will have opinions about opportunities based on their analysis of customer spending habits, which categories need more oomph, and how your profitability is shaping up against targets.

Marketing: These folks will have tons of valuable information around which campaigns drove sales and which fell flat. They can see what topics your competitors are lifting up in their digital campaigns and where the opportunities are based on the big picture.

And since we're talking about your competition again and all the learnings available there, keep in mind that they can also be a great motivator to come up with your own fresh ideas—you know: do what they are doing, but better! And don't forget to factor in time to keep up to date with the latest magazines, books, cooking shows, blogs, TikToks, and anything else food related. Food culture is constantly shifting and evolving, and if you don't look up from your spreadsheets every once in a while, you're going to be left behind.

And, of course, *you* are your own source of inspiration—so have a notepad handy and listen to yourself, always. But keep in mind that the greatest development leaders ensure their *teams* are lifted up and that their ideas are put front and center. An engaged and motivated team will deliver incredible performance—which means your job is to remove roadblocks from their path and make their success your priority. Everybody wins that way. Plus, it's way more fun.

IT'S TIME TO GET INTO MISE MODE

You might be able to build one great new recipe with your eye just on the kitchen, but you definitely need to engage every area of your business to create a complete menu design strategy—and to make it go off without a hitch.

1. Use your Mise Mode Launch Timeline to schedule out your launch from at least 13 weeks in advance.

2. Make sure to consider the integral role each team (or team member or business focus, if you are an independent owner or operator and are doing it with few or no people) will play in the launch of your new menu, from sourcing to team training.

3. Communicate regularly with *everyone*—both within and apart from your launch schedule. Each member of your team has unique, valuable insights, including your outside vendors. Don't leave that gold sitting on the table.

Hi! Did you watch the quick tutorials for the tools?

5

CARE FOR A CASE STUDY?

The Life and Death of a Lil' Dippie

I'M NOT GOING TO KEEP YOU in suspense: a hero dies at the end of this story. Sometimes you can have an amazing menu item idea that both hits the spot *and* fills a gap, you can work at the recipe until the numbers show a healthy profit, you can get all your colleagues on board and scheduled out perfectly in your Mise Mode Launch Timeline, and still see the knees knocked out from under it right in the final stretch. Friends, let me introduce you to the Lil' Dippie.

While this product failed to make it to market, it still stands as an excellent case study that brings all of the considerations you've read about so far into one timeline. And, really, all the better if it never actually made it onto a menu, because that's a fine example of those unknown unknowns that can hit you from behind—because they're going to come, and you're going to have to learn how to dust yourself off and move on when they do.

Okay, so: What the heck is a Lil' Dippie? *I'm so glad you asked!* I grew up eating traditional French dip sandwiches with my dad and I always loved the experience of getting a warm pastrami sandwich with a massive layer of gooey-melty Jack cheese, all smothered in "double dip" jus and eaten with super spicy mustard and way too many pickles on the side. My dad and I would go to a restaurant called Philippe's in LA (where there was sawdust was all over the floor for some odd but super fun reason). The sandwiches were served with a small pot of extra warm and scrumptious "au jus," and my dad and I would just sit there and dip away. The warm French roll was equal parts crisp and soppy-soggy, and it was a bit like eating a sloppy, toasty, meaty, happy mess—in short, the absolutely perfect interactive eating experience for a dad-and-daughter meal. I just adored them.

So when I was leading development and saw an opportunity to introduce a sandwich influenced by this classic "French-dip" experience, I put my team right to work. We used every menu planning tool available—our category spreadsheets, our development calendars, our costing calculators, our launch timelines—and developed a selection of warm, portable, totally awesome sandwiches that came with a choice of sides to use for dipping: either a delicious "homemade" gravy, molasses baked beans, or maple syrup for those who like it sweet.

Sounds great, right? Well, in the long run it *was* great—because now I get to turn it into a real-world example of how to put this entire Mise Mode menu planning framework into action.

Framework Step 1: Brand Integrity

This particular concept focused on healthy, easy, classic, and reasonably affordable. With a mind to our food principles, nutritional goals, and pricing targets—plus the desire to offer an interactive eating experience—we came up with five individual product options for the category similar to these:

- Turkey, Stuffing, and Spiced Cranberry Chutney with Turkey Gravy
- Black Pepper Roast Beef with Old School Au Jus
- Roasted Cardamom Apple Toast with Ricotta and Warm Maple Syrup
- Roast Chicken Classic with Chicken Gravy
- Egg, Sausage, and Tomato with Slow-Cooked Molasses Baked Beans

The idea behind these different variations was to explore different meal periods, and to give the purchasing team enough options to work with that we would meet our target launch date. (We didn't know yet how hard it would be to source the specific styles of sliced bread and gravy that would meet our unique food principle specifications—more on that later.)

Framework Step 2: Seasonality

Given the characteristics of this new product category—a fun and interactive hot sandwich dipping experience, we planned to launch it in winter, when the weather gets cold and diners get excited about having something delicious and toasty to enjoy. (Not to mention the arrival of Thanksgiving, when we all lose our nostalgic little minds for gravy.) I started to plot out our development schedule to deliver this new product range and ensure we had enough time to test and tweak it so that it was a smooth launch beginning to end.

Framework Step 3: Money

We started to pull together the recipe costing sheets to see what we could do with the price points while keeping our margins intact. There were plating and packaging considerations to nail down, too, and we had a lot of work to do to come up with realistic projections for how many Lil' Dippies our customers would purchase during the time these products would be listed on the menus. As we started getting pricing information from our purchasing team on the different options with different pack sizes, we started to see a clear vision of which of the product options were going to be too expensive to execute, and which would work well.

We already had a sense of what would be possible on the operations side—we had just launched a new type of grill in our restaurants and were actively collaborating with the front-line managers and team members to ensure high quality execution with this new equipment. We had high hopes for these heating tools, and they were a big factor in why we decided to move forward with developing a lot of new hot food items.

Hiccup Time: Supply Chain Challenges

These delicious little dipped numbers required us to find a supplier who could make an enormous amount of wonderful gravy using the same cooking techniques that your grandma might have used at home. You know—using actual roasted turkey bones, real veggie trimmings, and thickening the gravy with butter and flour or (in a pinch) cornstarch.

We also needed a vendor with the ability to not only make the gravy at high volumes, but also to cool it down safely, package it for fresh transport, and ship it across the country without freezing it, all while ensuring the shelf life had enough legs that it could actually be used before it expired. Fresh, satisfying old-school gravy, with no preservatives or any weird crap in there. A tall order, I'm sorry to say.

Luckily, we had an incredible soup supplier who already made totally awesome "homemade" soups for us, and they had the operational capabilities to produce just what we needed. Hooray! To give you an idea of what their commercial kitchen looked like, imagine the biggest pot you own at home, and then super-size it to the scale of a large, deep jacuzzi. Then, imagine a whole room of these jacuzzi-sized cooking pots, all bubbling away at the same time with a bunch of different soups. *Soup heaven.* We asked them if they could make a gravy for us, and they came back with a wonderful, high-quality roast turkey gravy that met all of our operational, sourcing, and food principle requirements. Things were looking great once again!

Framework Step 4: Operations (and Our Next Hiccup)

With the help of our launch timeline, we had ticked off all the boxes for recipe build and execution, storage and handling of products, and the sourcing and supply chain. We were well underway. But! We still had one wild card. Testing the performance of that new grill to make sure those bad boys would be perfectly perfect every single time.

That's the thing about menu development: you never know where you're going to find your next challenge. It won't be in the same place as it was last time, but it will be there somewhere. *Always.* Your job as a menu development strategist is to determine where the risk points are and ensure those potential bottlenecks are solved for *before* you move forward with a committed launch. The last thing you want to do is blow up your operations and impact your guest experience with a product that cannot be executed within a reasonable time frame, or to the quality standards you demand... Every. Single. Time.

And you will also find yourself needing to really push people to get them on board. The reality is that most people have an allergic reaction to change—I talk a lot about this in *A Taste of Opportunity*—and sometimes, when faced with some new operational challenge, their first and even second reaction is to say "nope." Being in operations *and* being a chef really helped me understand where the line was when I was pressing for a new item, and when to back off. I believe in the capacity of people to deliver products they are excited about even when it means they have to work differently (read: harder). But sometimes you *are* going to meet brick walls—over time, you'll learn how hard you can safely hammer at them.

In the case of the Lil' Dippies, it turned out that the new grill was not performing the way we thought it would—heating them up was creating a dangerous time lag in for our service team, causing longer waits for customers. Still, we kept hammering, trying to find a solution.

Knowing When It's Time to Say Goodbye

There are a great many reasons why a spectacular product that ticks every box in the development process never sees the light of day. Sometimes a menu item will do well in a testing store, but there are simply too many competing priorities across the larger company to put resources into scaling it up. Sometimes it needed a champion at the executive level but you just couldn't get the right people interested—or worse, it had an antagonist who, for whatever reason, didn't like the idea and actively worked to kill it. (Corporate politics are real!) Sometimes, it's a simple operational roadblock that you just can't get around, no matter how hard you try.

In the case of the Lil' Dippie, it wasn't just the grill that killed it, it was also a storage issue that we should have foreseen but didn't. When a restaurant only has so much square footage available, that means all of your refrigerated, frozen, and dry goods will be competing for room. So, for each item you want to bring into the system, you are going to need to either kick something else out the door, or find ways to use a few things in multiple ways to increase that space efficiency. And even if you do solve your storage issues, you're going to have to think through the *handling*: how exactly you are going to get that product into your customers' hands—and what might need to be sacrificed to do so.

As it turns out, the gravy that we had been so excited to procure was going to create yet another operational bottleneck. With our existing lineup of soups already competing for countertop space, which soup option would we have to kill to make space for this simmering gravy? Combine that with the too-slow grill and the Lil' Dippie was simply not viable. Think about it: in a high-volume environment where a typical transaction was taking under a minute, imagine how long it would take to execute a dozen Lil' Dippies or more at once—factoring in toasting, gravy ladling, packaging, and purchase transaction. What if a customer came in and ordered four to take back to the office? And what if 20 people wanted one all at once?

So even though we wanted to expand our category of hot menu items, and even though the Lil' Dippie passed every test we had put it through to that point, we ended up dumping it in the "needs equipment innovation and upgrades" pile. Remember the end scene of *Raiders of the Lost Ark*, when the forklift takes the boxed-up ark of the covenant that everyone had fought so hard for and drives it way, way back to the far, far reaches of a massive warehouse to gather dust for eternity? That's what this pile is in the restaurant business. So, the Lil' Dippie pretty much got lost in space. I'm not going to lie: I'm still bummed about it. But who knows—you may still see something like this pop up in your life some day! Maybe even before you get to the end of this book! Heck, anything is possible.

And meanwhile, for every sandwich that doesn't make it, there's a different hero out there (was that another food pun?) that will. So if you create a menu darling that you end up needing to kill, just open up those Mise Mode spreadsheets and try, try again.

IT'S TIME TO GET INTO MISE MODE

You have to expect the unexpected in the food industry—sometimes everything can go right and it can all still turn out wrong. Here are your best strategies for staying nimble and getting back on your feet.

1. Your food principles are going to create roadblocks you might not expect. Hold the line—it's better to change your menu plan than sacrifice your values—and your brand integrity.

2. Test, test, and retest at every stage of the process. Have you heard the saying about a butterfly wing causing a hurricane? Each change you make in your menu is going to cause ramifications somewhere else. Don't let them come as a surprise.

3. Be like Elsa from *Frozen* and, when you have to, let it go. Sometimes a menu item you love just can't get over the line. Who knows. Maybe you'll get to use it in a book someday.

Here it is again! The QR code to your menu planning dreams!

A CLOSING NOTE
WHY WHAT YOU PUT ON YOUR MENU REALLY, *REALLY* MATTERS

SO, NOW THAT YOU EXPERIENCED this little window into the world of high-volume, fresh food menu development and what it takes to launch something new into the marketplace, I hope you have a clearer understanding of what it really takes to get a delicious recipe from your mind into customer hands—successfully. And all of these many challenges and considerations are super-sized for those of us who want to provide the world with food that follows a defined set of values—whether that's about health, affordability, access, fair labor, wage parity, transparency, sustainability, animal welfare, or any other food-related matter that is important to you and your business. (And, really, aren't *all* matters food related?) Food development is expensive. It takes the right strategies and the right tools, and it takes time. We have to have stamina and persistence to change ingrained systems. So much can go wrong, at any stage of the process. And still we do it. Why? *Because we love food, and we love delighting, inspiring, connecting, and nourishing people through food experiences.*

As a person who is building your career around providing people with that connection and nourishment, you have a lot of power—and a lot of responsibility. Our food systems have become so complicated and our production processes so, well, *artificial*, because food businesses at every link in the supply, production, and sales chain want to make their items last longer, travel farther, cost less, and sell for more. Yes, these are all critical issues for any business, but they are absolutely not what is best for us as a society in the long run, in my humble opinion.

That is the message I want to leave you with. Yes, financial viability is important. Yes, doing the right thing is often way harder and way more expensive. But we are all capable of navigating these complexities and rising to the challenge of producing menus with fresh, real food in reasonable portion sizes designed to support human and environmental health. We cannot and should not settle for the status quo just because it's easier or cheaper or more profitable. Staying purposefully driven to improve food production and execution processes (by demanding them) and delivering better nutrition to more people should be a shared goal for all of us in this industry.

With that said, progress is progress and we should take a moment to celebrate the fact that we as an industry are having conversations about food in ways we never have before. Consumers are more curious about where their food comes from and how it is prepared, and those new values in transparency are reshaping the next generation of food producers, manufacturers, restaurants, and retailers across the country and around the world. It's awesome to witness, and I can't wait to see where those conversations will take us next. And where *you* will take us next!

We need people in the industry at the highest levels of leadership who understand the significance of this remarkable opportunity to connect, inspire, and influence our communities through food "for the betterment of everyone." My call to action for you is that you take a moment to think about how you can ultimately influence your organization to transform our world for the better while you put these tools and strategies into action.

I'm behind you, beside you, and rooting for you, always!

Spiced-Apple French Toast (for on the GO!)

SERVES 2 HUNGRY EATERS

Have I left you dreaming of my beloved Lil' Dippies? Here's a recipe for a very dippable hand-held hot breakfast that—while it's not exactly the same—will get you close enough to the Lil' Dippie vibe to know why I loved that recipe so much... it's interactive, warm, satisfying, fun to eat, and totally scrumptious.

If you're eating it at home or at work, put this baby on a plate with a small dipping cup of maple syrup. If you're "on the go," wrap the French toast in parchment paper and place the syrup in a portable, sealed container. You don't want to miss a drop of that liquid gold!

---

4 brioche slices, 1- to 1½-inch thick
You can get creative here with a brioche flavored with spices, dried fruits, nuts, even chocolate!

4 Granny Smith apples (or tart apples of your choice), diced with the cores removed

3 tablespoons salted butter, divided

1 tablespoon brown sugar
Dark or light is fine, depending on whatcha got and/or your mood

½ teaspoon cinnamon, ground

2 eggs, mixed well in a bowl

1 cup whole milk

1½ cups ricotta cheese, divided

½ cup pure maple syrup
Don't even think about cheating here. Corn syrup masquerading as maple syrup is just gross, so do it right and get the good stuff—you won't regret it, I promise!

Slice your bread and set aside. Add the eggs, whole milk, and ½ cup of the ricotta to a bowl and whisk well.

Add 1 tablespoon butter to a sauté pan on medium heat. Sauté the apples with brown sugar and cinnamon until softened. Place in a bowl and set aside.

Add the remaining 2 tablespoons butter to the pan and melt over medium-high heat.

While the butter is melting, add the brioche slices to the egg mixture and generously soak it up. Once the butter is sizzling in the pan, add the soaked brioche and sauté until golden brown. Flip and repeat until both sides are golden brown. Now you have French toast! Remove it from the heat.

Place the 4 browned French toast slices on a plate (or parchment paper if eating "on the go"). Add ½ cup of ricotta to two of the slices.

Spread the sautéed apples evenly over the ricotta, then close the sandwiches with the remaining 2 slices of bread. Add maple syrup to a small cup (or takeaway container) and serve warm and ready to eat. Enjoy!

There are so many variations you can make of this—from berry compotes to fruit sautés (such as pears or an apple/raisin/currant mix). Anything you think sounds delicious probably will be, so just go for it!

TOOLS AND RESOURCES

NOW THAT YOU SEE the big picture, it's time to get into Mise Mode and start developing your own menu strategy. Use the link below to download all of these Mise Mode planning templates that you can easily customize to your own business needs:

- Mise Mode Food Launch Timeline
- Annual Holiday Development Calendar
- Annual Product Development Calendar
- Menu Item Category Organizer
- Recipe Cost Calculator
- Competitors' Product Review Tracker
- Job Aide Training Sheet
- And more!

You can also find all of these templates and more at **essayerfoodconsulting.com**.

Last chance to grab them!

Where to Go From Here?

We've got a lot more to talk about!

First of all, you can find me on LinkedIn, Instagram, or Twitter **@GuilbaultRenee**—come and say hi! I would love to hear from you!

Need more support?

If you or your team need help getting your menu design system built out and ready to roll, not to worry! We have different support packages available to help you get your menu system designed and implemented— just head over to **essayerfoodconsulting.com** to find out more.

Essayer and the kickass Mise Mode Team provide consulting, training, and resources for Restaurants, CPG, DTC, and Independent Food Operators, so you can focus on what matters most...

Growing your career, your team, and your business!

ABOUT THE AUTHOR

RENEE GUILBAULT is a veteran food-industry consultant and author with expertise in large-scale, global, multi-unit food and beverage operations. Now principal of Essayer Food Consulting, she has held leadership roles at Pret A Manger, Bon Appétit Management Company at Google, Compass Group, and Le Pain Quotidien, where she was instrumental in developing revolutionary menus and executing high-volume strategies all over the world. Her book, *A Taste of Opportunity: An Insider's Guide to Boosting Your Career, Making Your Mark, and Changing the Food Industry from Within*, focuses on the abundant, often little-known, career opportunities within the trillion-dollar food industry that exist for anyone, from any walk of life (regardless of background or educational achievements), and combines her personal story of climbing the ladder with first-hand career and leadership insights from a truly exceptional group of 15 global food experts. Today, Renee lives in Boston with her family.

www.ingramcontent.com/pod-product-compliance
Lightning Source LLC
Chambersburg PA
CBHW020132130526
44590CB00040B/580